Science Builders

# ROBOTICS
## ENGINEERING

### LEARN IT, TRY IT!

Ed Sobey

Raintree is an imprint of Capstone Global Library Limited, a company incorporated in England and Wales having its registered office at 264 Banbury Road, Oxford, OX2 7DY – Registered company number: 6695582

www.raintree.co.uk
myorders@raintree.co.uk

Edited by Mandy Robbins
Designed by Steve Mead
Picture research by Kelli Lageson
Production by Laura Manthe
Originated by Capstone Global Library Limited
Printed and bound in India

ISBN 978 1 474 74065 4 (hardback)
21 20 19 18 17
10 9 8 7 6 5 4 3 2 1

ISBN 978 1 474 74069 2 (paperback)
22 21 20 19 18
10 9 8 7 6 5 4 3 2 1

British Library Cataloguing in Publication Data
A full catalogue record for this book is available from the British Library.

Acknowledgements
We would like to thank the following for permission to reproduce photographs: Capstone Studio: Karon Dubke, cover (bottom right), back cover (right), 14, 15 (top and bottom), 16 (all), 17, 18, 19, 20, 21 (top and bottom), 22, 24, 25 (top and bottom), 26, 27, 30 (top and bottom), 31 (top and bottom), 32 (all), 33 (all), 36, 37 (all); Shutterstock: 5, 7, ajt, 13 (bottom), asharkyu, 4, 28, Bplanet, 13 (top), cepera, cover (background), Cylonphoto, 39, Dennis Rozie, 10, DGLimages, 44, Dmytro Zinkevych, cover (top left), Elena Hramova, 11, Ivaschenko Roman, 13 (middle), Janaka Dharmasena, 38, Mariusz S. Jurgielewicz, 8, Nick Kinney, cover (design element), Ociacia, cover (top right), 40, Olga Miltsova, 6, Prasit Rodphan, 35, risteski goce, cover (bottom left), Savgraf, cover, Thanapun, 9, Triff, 34, tulpahn, 41, 42

# CONTENTS

# CHAPTER 1

# IDEAS IN MOTION

Would you recognize a robot if you saw one? Can you say exactly what a robot is? Robots are machines that move and are controlled by computers. Robots allow you to physically control objects and gadgets using a computer. Many machines are controlled by computers. So what makes robots different? Unlike most machines, robots can do more than one task. Their movements are a result of programming. They can move and do things on their own. They can even communicate. But they can't think.

Robotics engineers write the computer programs that tell robots what to do. Engineers can make robots do almost anything. Robotics engineers can change the **code** of the computer inside a robot. Then the robot performs different actions. A robot that paints cars could be programmed to paint each car a different colour. When the factory makes a different model of car, the painting robot can be reprogrammed to paint the new model. Robotics engineers need two important skills – computer programming and a knack for building things.

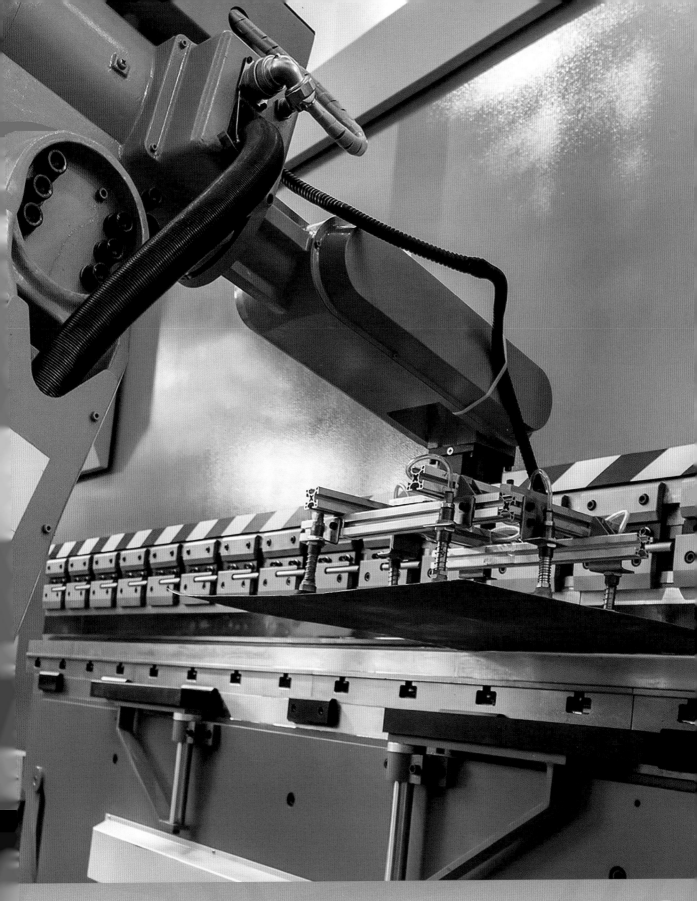

**code** system of words, letters, symbols or numbers used instead of ordinary words to send messages or store information; computer code serves as instructions for a computer

## IS THIS A ROBOT?

You may be surprised by what is technically considered a robot and what is not. Take a look at the machines around you. Do any of them qualify as robots?

Is a typical vacuum cleaner a robot? It is a machine. It collects dirt from the floor into a bag or container. But can you change what it does? Not easily. You would have to rebuild the machine so it could do something different. There is no computer inside.

Although most vacuum cleaners are not robots, some are. They clean a floor without a person doing anything other than turning them on. Some can be programmed for different cleaning patterns or carpets.

Robotic vacuum cleaners change direction when they hit something larger than they are.

What about a remote-controlled car? Do you think that is a robot? It follows your commands, even if you are standing at the other side of the room. You may be surprised to learn that a remote-controlled car is not a robot. Though some robots do have remote controls, they also have internal computers and programs. A remote-controlled car doesn't. Because it doesn't have a computer, it can't be reprogrammed to do other tasks.

A remote-controlled car can't do anything without a human controlling it.

Once a robot has been designed and built it can be controlled by a computer from any distance. Robotics engineers are creating many new ways to control robots. Some are experimenting with sending commands over the internet. This process is called the "internet of things". With this method, you could control a robot at home while you are on holiday far away.

# A SHORT HISTORY OF ROBOTS

The first programmable machine was a loom called the Jacquard loom. Its designer, Joseph Marie Jacquard, first demonstrated it in 1801. The pattern of the cloth being woven could be changed or programmed. The program was encoded on blocks of wood. The loom followed the instructions on the blocks. Today we use computers to write and store codes for robots.

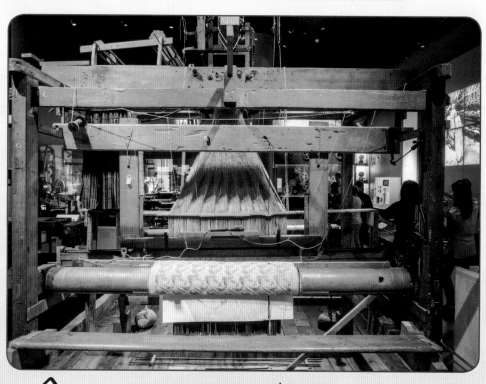

⬆ The Jacquard loom made it easy to weave complex patterns into cloth.

The word "robot" was first used in the 1920 play *R.U.R.* (standing for *Rossum's Universal Robots*). In the play, a man makes a robot to do his boring work. Robots are great at that. Once you have programmed a robot to do a job, it can continue to do it as long as it has electrical power to operate. But in this story, the robots revolted against humans.

In the last 100 years, many new technologies have been invented that make it easier to build and control robots. Electronic **circuits** are much smaller and much more capable. This allows robots to do more jobs and be reprogrammed quickly. **Sensors** that detect light, sound, objects and chemicals help robots to do more advanced work. Electric motors have advanced so much that robots can now perform surgery or move heavy objects. Lighter and stronger materials have also been invented to give robots strength without weighing them down.

# Challenge

Can you write a story about a robot? What powers will your robot have? What sort of work will it do? Can you write a good description of your robot and how it works? How would you go about building that robot in real life?

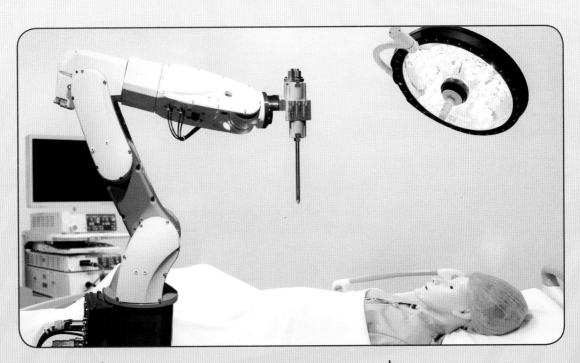

⬆ Medical robots perform work very precisely.

# CHAPTER 2

# ROBOTS IN MOTION

A robot begins with a frame. A robot's frame is called a platform. For small robots the platform is often made of stiff cardboard, plastic or wood. Larger robots often have metal platforms.

Many different parts can attach to a robot's platform. But what parts should you use? That depends on what you want your robot to do. If you want your robot to move, it will probably need wheels. Most cars have four wheels, but many robots have three. Two wheels drive the robot and the third wheel helps with balance. Some mobile robots use tracks over wheels such as those that bulldozers have. The tracks can give the robot great grip on slippery surfaces.

Wheels and tracks help robots to move, but they need motors to drive them. Motors **convert** electrical energy into motion. You can make a robot with one motor, but it's often easier to control a robot with two motors. Unlike a car, which has a steering wheel and one engine to propel it, robots typically have no steering wheel. Steering comes from operating the motors at different speeds. One motor turns one drive wheel or track. The second motor turns the second drive wheel or track. If the two motors spin at the same rate, the robot travels in a straight line. But if one motor spins faster than the other, the robot turns. If one motor spins backwards while the other spins forwards, the robot turns around in a circle.

Robots are sometimes built and used to compete in games. Different actions score points.

**1**

There are many types of motors that can be used for robotics. The projects presented in this book use low-**voltage** toy motors. They run on batteries. There are two wire connections from the motor to a battery or battery pack. There is no on/off switch for this type of motor. The instant a toy motor is connected to an electrical source, its motor starts running.

**2**

Engineers often use another type of motor called a servo motor. A servo motor is connected to a battery pack with two wires. When servo motors are connected to a power source, they don't spin. Servo motors have a third wire that serves as an on/off switch. So the first two wires provide power to the servo motor, and the third wire turns the motor on and off. Servo motors make it easy to control a robot's motion with a computer.

**3**

A third type of motor used in robots is the stepper motor. When this motor receives instructions to move, it powers the robot to move a small distance or take a "step". To go far, they take many tiny steps quickly. The robot's computer program directs it when to take steps. This type of motor lets a robot perform very precise tasks. Both paper and 3-D printers use stepper motors, as do high-quality camera lenses.

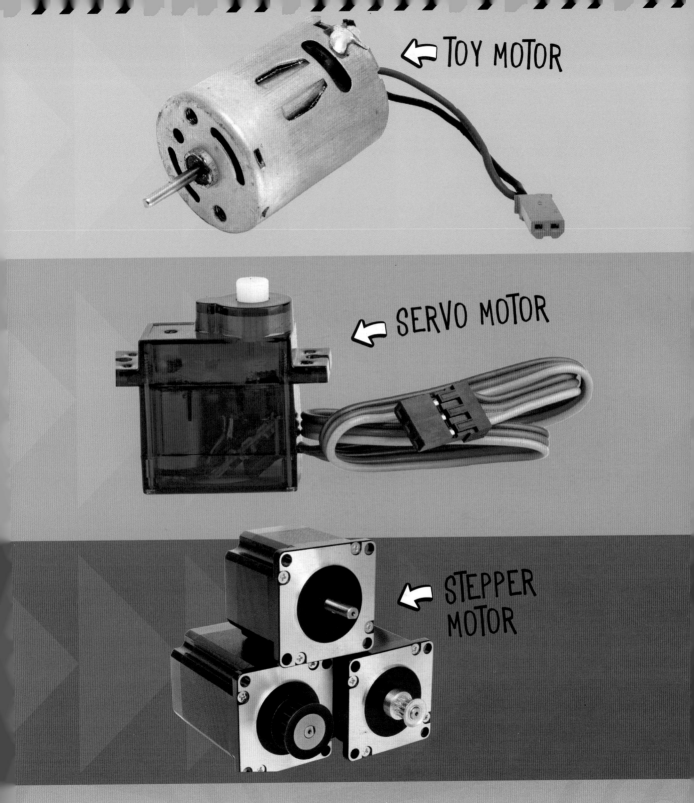

TOY MOTOR

SERVO MOTOR

STEPPER MOTOR

**voltage** force of an electrical current; voltage is measured in volts

# MAKE SOME MOTION

To get a robot to move you need to provide power to a motor. Give this simple project a try so that you know how to supply your robot with electricity.

## MATERIALS

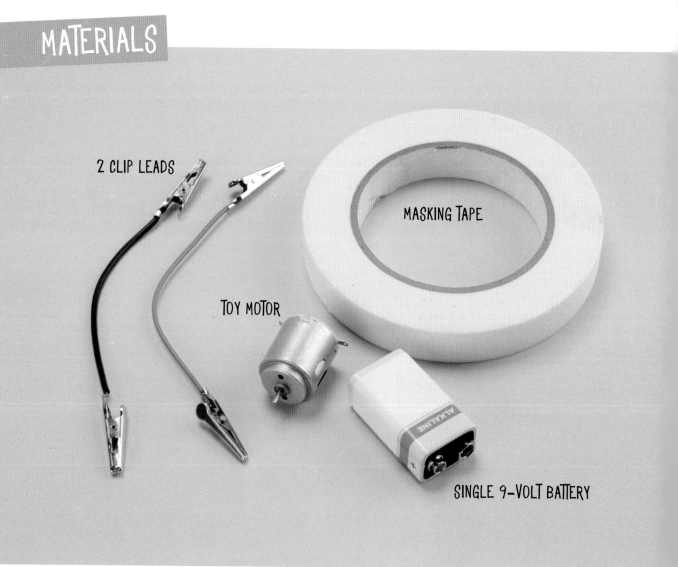

2 CLIP LEADS

MASKING TAPE

TOY MOTOR

SINGLE 9-VOLT BATTERY

Clip leads are wires that have spring clasps at each end. With clip leads you can easily connect a motor to a battery. The items you need for this project can be found online or in craft or hobby shops. Make sure you ask an adult to help you get your materials.

STEPS

1   Clip one of the leads to one of the two terminals on the battery.

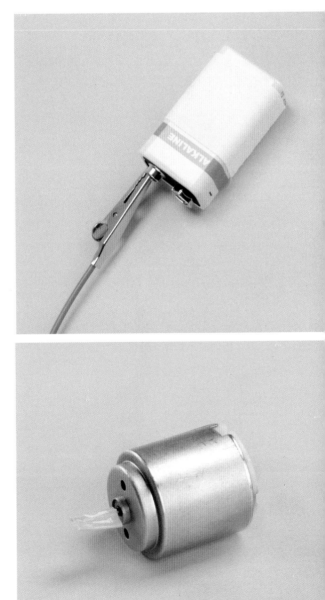

2   Find the motor shaft on the toy motor. The shaft is the metal rod sticking out from the centre of the motor. When the motor is running, the shaft spins. Fold a short piece of masking tape so it sticks to itself and to the shaft. This will help you to see the shaft spinning.

**3** Connect the other end of the clip lead to one of the terminals on the motor.

**4** Now connect the second clip lead between the remaining terminals on the battery and the motor. Your motor will jump to life!

## CAUTION:
Use only the batteries listed for the projects in this book. The electricity from wall sockets is much too powerful and dangerous.

5   The masking tape should be spinning. You've made a complete
    circuit, allowing **electrons** to flow from the battery through the
    clip leads to the motor and back to the battery.

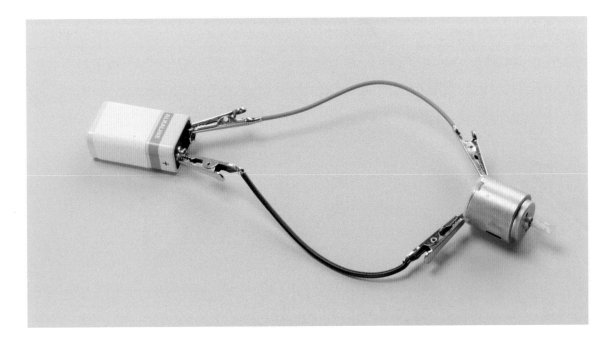

## Challenge

What direction is the tape spinning? When driving a mobile robot forwards, a motor will spin in one direction. To drive the robot in the opposite direction you must change the direction the motor is spinning. Can you get the motor to spin the other way? You will need to change the direction electrons are flowing through the circuit. How can you do this? Test your idea.

### HINT

It has something to do with the way you've attached your clip leads.

# BUILD A MOBILE PLATFORM

Now that you know how to power a motor, you can build the basis for a moving robot. This is called a mobile platform. You'll need the battery and motor from your first project, along with a few more items.

## MATERIALS

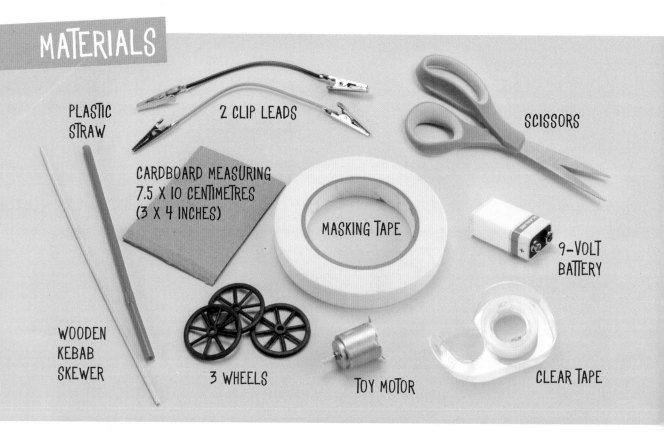

PLASTIC STRAW

2 CLIP LEADS

SCISSORS

CARDBOARD MEASURING 7.5 X 10 CENTIMETRES (3 X 4 INCHES)

MASKING TAPE

9-VOLT BATTERY

WOODEN KEBAB SKEWER

3 WHEELS

TOY MOTOR

CLEAR TAPE

Most of the items for this project can be found online or at craft or hobby shops. Some shops or websites will sell wheels and motors that easily fit together. You could also make your own wheels out of plastic bottle tops, or you could take the wheels off your old toys.

1   Cut a 7.5-centimetre (3-inch) length of straw.

2   Tape the straw across one end of the cardboard.

3   Cut a notch in the centre of the other end of the cardboard. Make the notch big enough so that one wheel can just fit in.

**4** Secure one wheel onto the shaft of the motor. If the shaft is too big for the hole, ask an adult to help widen the hole. If the hole is much larger than the motor shaft, wrap a piece of masking tape around the shaft. Try pushing the wheel onto the shaft. Adjust the amount of tape on the shaft until the wheel fits snugly.

**5** Tape the motor onto the cardboard rectangle. Position the wheel on the motor shaft so that it fits in the notch you cut in the cardboard.

**6** Cut the skewer to 10 centimetres (4 inches) long, and slide it through the straw. The straw serves as a **bearing**. The bearing holds the skewer, but lets it spin. The skewer will be the **axle**.

7   Slide one wheel onto each end of the axle. Place a small wad of tape at the end of each axle so the wheels won't slide off.

8   Tape the battery onto the cardboard. It should be on the top of the platform, and the straw bearing should be on the bottom.

**bearing**   in machinery, a part that holds an axle in place while allowing it to spin

**axle**   rod that connects two or more wheels

9    Connect the battery to the motor terminals using two clip leads.

10   The wheel should be spinning. Place the platform on the ground and watch it go.

**When you connect the second clip lead to the other motor terminal, your car will zoom off!**

Cars work better with front-wheel drive when they are on slippery surfaces. That means the motor powers the wheels at the front of the car. Look at your mobile platform. How does this relate to it? If your platform is driving with the motor at the back, try swapping it around. Swap the clip lead connections to the battery so that the motor spins in the other direction.

The wheel attached to the motor is called the drive wheel. If the drive wheel slips on the floor, try a floor with a different surface. You could also add a small weight above the wheel. Tape coins on to your platform to weigh it down. This will help the drive wheel to grip the floor.

Is your platform driving straight? If the platform turns to one side, compare the position of the axle to the motor shaft. Are they parallel? If not, the platform will not move in a straight line.

## Challenge

What can be done to make this model work better? That is a question robotics engineers ask themselves every day. Would having a second motor help? Would a smaller, lighter platform go faster? Set up a test track so you can measure how many seconds your platform takes to travel a short distance. Then change something on your platform and test it again. Try different wheels, a wider axle or any number of other changes. Keep a record of how fast your platform goes and improvements that make a difference.

# MAKE A JITTERBUG

## MANY WAYS TO MOVE

Wheels are great, but you don't have to use them to make a vehicle. Vehicles called hovercrafts don't have wheels. They blow air downwards so they can glide on a cushion of air. Skates and sledges have metal runners that slide across ice. Another way to travel without wheels is the jitterbug. It shakes to move. Each time it shakes, it jerks itself forwards.

Just as the vibrating mechanism inside a mobile phone shakes when a call is coming in, a vibrating motor on legs will jerk-step its way across a table. You can use the same type of motor as in your previous projects to make a jitterbug.

## MATERIALS

MASKING TAPE

SUPER GLUE

POLYSTYRENE CUP

9-VOLT BATTERY

PLASTIC ZIP TIE

4 CRAFT STICKS
OR PENCILS

TOY
MOTOR

2 CLIP LEADS

1. Secure the zip tie to the motor shaft. Ask an adult to help pull the end of the tie very tight so it will stay on. Put a drop of super glue onto the end of the shaft to help hold the zip tie in place.

2. Cut the zip tie so it is about 8 centimetres (3 inches) long.

3. Tape the four craft sticks onto the outside of the polystrene cup. Space them evenly around the cup. Place them so that half of each stick is touching the cup and the other half is projecting above the open end of the cup.

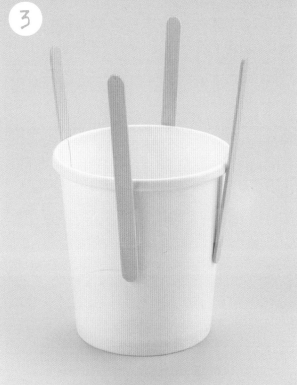

4 Tape the battery to the outside of the cup, as close to the rim as possible.

ALKALINE

5 Tape the motor to the bottom of the cup. The extra length of zip tie will stick out over the edge of the bottom. The motor and zip tie should be on the end opposite to the battery.

6  Connect the motor and battery with two clip leads. Your jitterbug should be moving. Stand it up to watch it shimmy across a table or floor.

**TIP**

If your jitterbug falls over, rearrange the battery and motor to balance the weight.

## CHANGES IN MOTION

Watch the motion of your jitterbug. You can change that motion in several different ways. First, add some weight to the jitterbug. Tape a few coins along the bottom of the cup. Note how the motion changed.

Next you can replace the battery with a battery pack holding two AA batteries. This substitution will make the motor spin slower. This will slow down the jumps. At slower motor speeds the jitterbug will be less jumpy.

One other option for changing the motion is to change the length of the zip tie. The simplest thing to do is to cut the zip tie shorter. Each time you shorten the zip tie, the motor speeds up, but the jerky motion decreases.

You could also add weight to the zip tie. Try taping a bead or small stone to the zip tie. Even a small weight will make a big change in the jitterbug's motion. Be careful to secure the weight very well. The rapid spinning will tend to rip it off the zip tie and send it flying across the room.

# CHAPTER 3

# ROBOTS MOVE THINGS

Mobile robots move themselves. But some robots stay still while moving other things. Factories use these types of robots to build cars, computers and telephones. They also use robots to paint things.

Think of something as simple as picking up a wad of crumpled paper. You can do it easily, but how could you get a machine to do it? This is the type of question robotics engineers face. When dealing with a challenge such as this, engineers often think of how a human or other animal would do it.

## ROBOTS IN THE WORKPLACE

People have invented machines to make their lives easier for thousands of years. Some robots are advanced machines that can do repetitive jobs all day. Robots in factories perform some jobs that people used to do. Some of those jobs are repetitive, and some are dangerous. Others require great precision. This type of accuracy is easy for a robot to repeat day after day, but it might be difficult for a person to do.

Robotics engineers and industrial engineers keep factory robots working and reprogram them for new jobs. When a factory's product or job changes, the robots can be reprogrammed to make a new product or perform a new task.

↑

Factories use arm robots
to do precision work.

# MAKE A HAND

Your hand is a great model for a robotic grabber. See if you can replicate it. What makes fingers effective at grabbing things? Think about what's inside them. They have bones, joints and two sets of muscles. One set of muscles closes the fingers and another opens them. The muscles are connected to the bones. The bones are connected to each other.

## MATERIALS

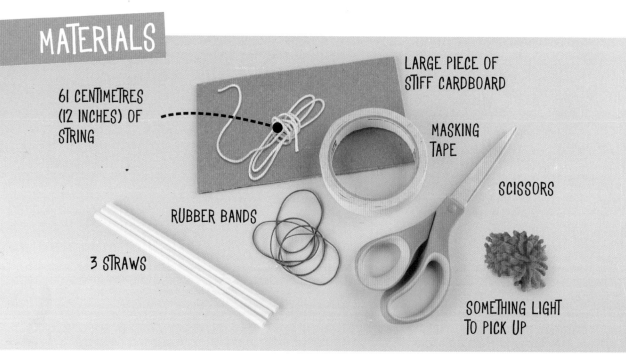

61 CENTIMETRES (12 INCHES) OF STRING

LARGE PIECE OF STIFF CARDBOARD

MASKING TAPE

SCISSORS

RUBBER BANDS

3 STRAWS

SOMETHING LIGHT TO PICK UP

## STEPS

1. Cut two strips of cardboard measuring 2.5 x 15 centimetres (1 x 6 inches). These strips will act as a finger and thumb.

2    Bend each strip twice into three equal sections. The bends will serve as joints.

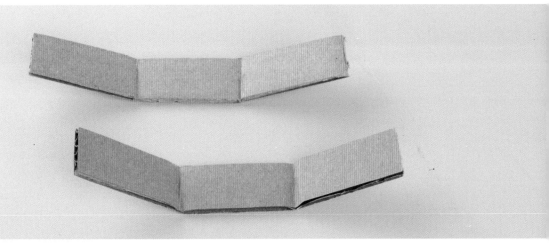

3   Cut six pieces of a straw. Make each piece a bit shorter than the straight sections of the cardboard from step 2. Tape the straw sections on to one flat side of the finger and thumb. Each cardboard strip should have three pieces of straw.

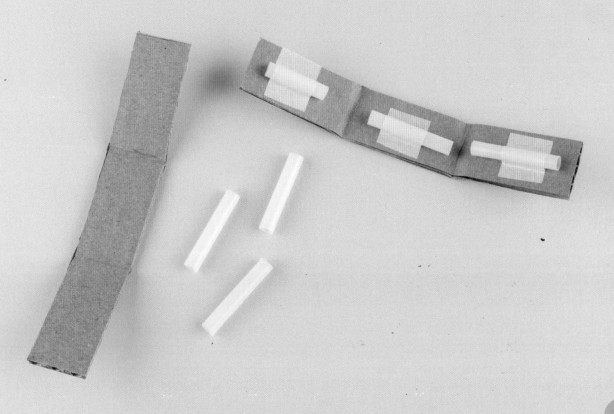

4 Tape one end of each cardboard strip to a larger piece of cardboard. This large piece is like the palm of a hand.

5 Slide a piece of string through the straws on the two cardboard strips. Tie or tape the end of the string to the tip of the finger and thumb.

6 Pull on the other end of the string to get the finger and thumb to close.

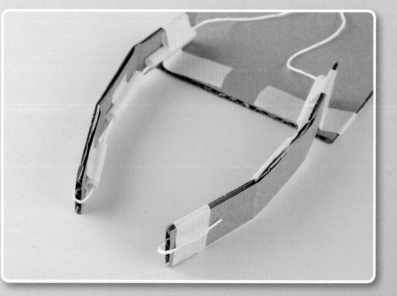

7   To get the grabber to open you will need something to pull the finger and thumb back. Rubber bands will work. Cut two rubber bands so that each is a single strand. Tape one end of a strand at each end of the finger and thumb. Adjust the **tension** on the rubber band so that the finger and thumb remain open unless the strings are pulled. When you have it right, tape the other end of the rubber band down.

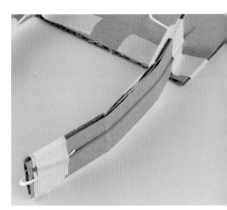

8   Pull the string to close the grabber. When you let go of the string, the rubber band should open the grabber.

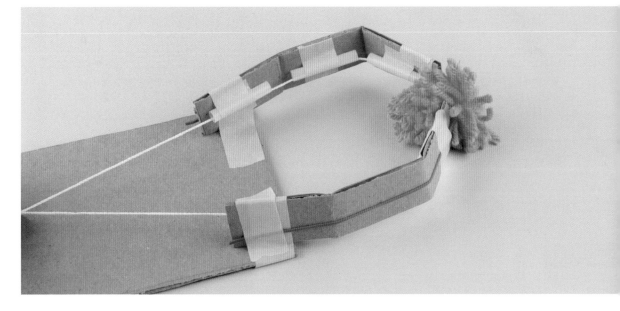

# Challenge

Some robots have hands to grasp things. They use motors to open and close the hands. But motors create spinning motion, not grabbing motion. Engineers convert the spinning motion to a back and forth motion. One way to do this is to use a motor to power a crank. Turning the crank closes and opens the hand. Draw a picture of your crank-powered hand.

# CHAPTER 4

# SENSORS

Most robots have sensors. Mobile robots may use sensors to detect conditions around them. Imagine a robot landing on Mars, for example. It should start searching the planet only when it's warm enough for the robot to function well. The robot reads a thermometer every few minutes. The thermometer is a sensor. When the temperature rises to the set number, the robot can start moving.

Some moving robots have two metal wires extending at the front. These are its "whiskers". They are touch sensors. They feel for objects in front of the robot. If the robot is about to run into a wall, one of the whiskers will brush against the wall. This touch sensor sends a signal to the robot's computer. The computer can then stop the motors so that the robot doesn't hit the wall.

↑ Robots in factories use sensors to do precision work quickly and accurately.

Whiskers or touch sensors are just one of many different types of sensors. Sensors that detect light can direct the robot towards or away from light. Other sensors send out a signal of light or sound. When the light or sound reflects off of a wall the robot's computer can calculate the distance to the wall.

# MAKE A SUN-CONTROLLED MOBILE PLATFORM

Try adding a sensor to your mobile platform. A solar panel is a sensor that detects bright sunlight. When it finds enough sunlight, the robot starts moving.

## MATERIALS

MASKING TAPE

CLIP LEADS

A SOLAR PANEL
(4.5 VOLTS)

MOBILE PLATFORM FROM PROJECT 2

Ask an adult to help you order a solar panel online. If you would like to do some other solar projects, buy at least two solar panels that can produce 4.5 volts of power or more.

1 Add the solar panel to the circuit for your mobile platform. The solar panel has a black wire and a red wire. The red wire is positive, and the black wire is negative. Connect the red wire to the negative side of the 9-volt battery. The battery will have positive and negative symbols.

2 Connect the solar panel's black wire to one of the motor terminals.

3 Use a clip lead to connect the positive terminal of the battery to the remaining terminal on the motor.

4 With the solar panel in direct sunlight, the motor and wheel should spin fast. Turn the solar panel upside down so sunlight doesn't hit it. The motor should stop.

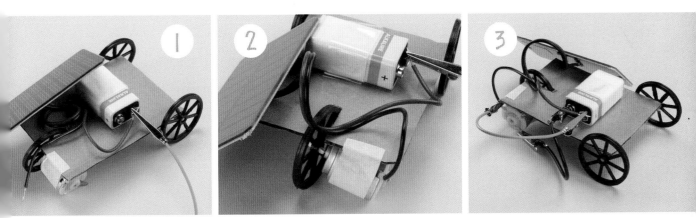

# Challenge

This project used a solar panel to allow electricity to pass through the circuit. Can you use the solar panel by itself to power the motor? Remove the battery and connect the solar panel to the motor. You should be able to wind the wires from the solar panel directly around your motor terminals. Hold the panel so it faces the sun. Does the drive wheel spin? If you need more power, try using two solar panels. Connect the red wire of one panel to the black wire of the second panel. Connect the other two panel wires to the motor.

# CHAPTER 5

# PROGRAMMING

Robots have two main parts – the machine and the computer. Most robots have computers called **microprocessors**. The microprocessor stores the program that directs the robot. It also sends on and off signals to the motors, lights and sound makers. If the robot has sensors, the microprocessor receives signals from them. Microprocessors are connected to the robot's circuit board. A circuit board has all of the electrical components that a robot needs to operate.

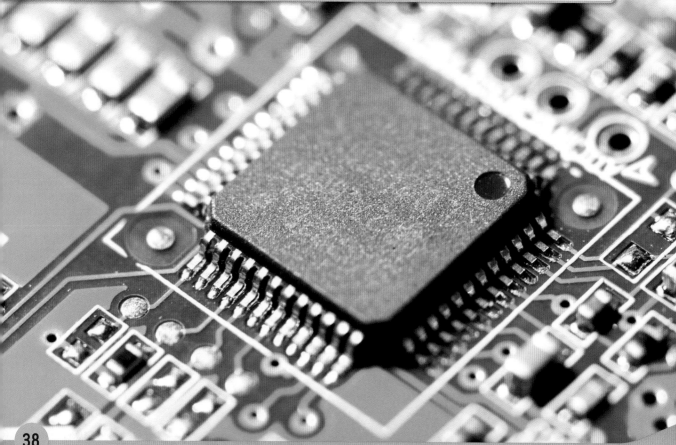

Each of a robot's programs is created on a larger computer. When the program is ready it is downloaded by a cable or sent wirelessly to the microprocessor. The microprocessor follows each step in the program. It controls motors, collects data from sensors and acts based on what the program tells it to do.

Imagine a robot trying to find its way through a maze. There are many ways to build such a robot. One is to use touch sensors. When one of the sensors touches a wall in the maze, it sends a signal to the microprocessor. The microprocessor might turn the motors in reverse to get it away from the wall. After backing away from the wall, the microprocessor might drive the robot in a new direction as it tries to find its way out of the maze.

⬆ A properly programmed robot could find its way out of a maze without human assistance.

# WRITE A PROGRAM

Microprocessors, like other computers, operate based on a code in the program. They follow an order of commands given to them.

Imagine you are going to program a robot through the maze on page 41. The red character is your robot. The black lines are the edges of the maze. The scale at the bottom shows how far the robot travels for each step. Use the code symbols provided. Can you write a code to get the robot into the maze and out the other side?

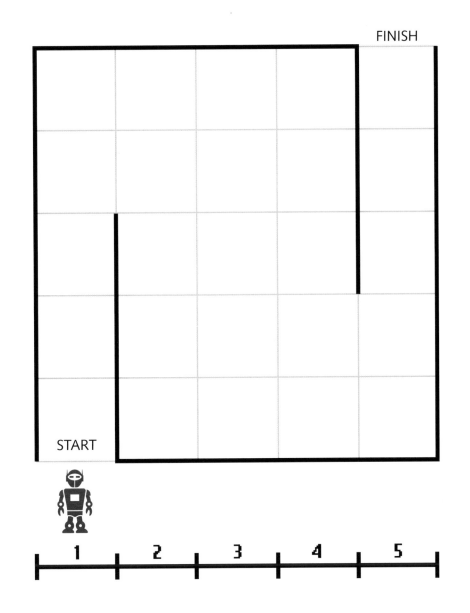

FINISH

START

1  2  3  4  5

## CODE SYMBOLS

| What you want the robot to do | Code command | |
|---|---|---|
| Go forwards one space | FOR | ↑ |
| Go backwards one space | BAC | ↓ |
| Turn left 90 degrees | LFT | ← |
| Turn right 90 degrees | RGT | → |

On a piece of paper write a code that will drive your robot.

Ask someone else to double-check your code to make sure it works.

## USING LOOPS

Each instruction for your robot is given one line of space. How many instructions, or lines of code, did you use?

**FOR**
**FOR**
**FOR**
**FOR**
**RGT**
**RGT**
**RGT**
**BAC**
**BAC**
**BAC**
**RGT**
**FOR**
**FOR**
**FOR**
**FOR**

|  | | | | FINISH |
|---|---|---|---|---|
|  | | | | **FOR** |
| **FOR** | **RGT** | **RGT** | **RGT** | **FOR** |
| **FOR** | | | **BAC** | **FOR** |
| **FOR** | | | **BAC** | **FOR** |
| **FOR** | | | **BAC** | **RGT** |
| START | | | | |

This particular example uses 15 lines of code. Each line of code takes up space in a program, and some microprocessors have small memories. To save space and to make the code easier to review, robotics engineers use shortcuts. One type of shortcut is called a loop. A loop allows engineers to use the same command many times. Rather than writing the command for "forwards" five times, they would use a loop. A loop begins with an instruction of how many times a command should be followed. Then the command is listed. On the final line the loop is closed with the instruction "Loop end".

These two programs do the same thing. The program on the right has one fewer line of code.

| CODE SYMBOLS | |
|---|---|
| **First program** | **Shorter program** |
| FOR | Do loop 5 times |
| FOR | FOR |
| FOR | Loop end |
| FOR | |

Imagine how many lines of code you would save if the robot had to move 300 steps instead of 5. Now try rewriting the code to get your robot through the maze. This time use loops.

## Challenge

If you've programmed your robot out of this simple maze, try making your own maze. Add more lines to make it more complicated. Challenge your friends to make complex mazes and then write the code to get through them.

## THE PATH TO ENGINEERING

If you have made the models described in this book, you are ready for the next step. Look for a robotics kit you can assemble and program. There are many kits available for building programmable robots. Having a programmable robot gives you endless possibilities for what you would like it to do. You can rebuild the hardware or recode the software to make any changes you want. When you're a robotics engineer there is always something new to learn and build.

And you don't have to do all of your experimenting on your own. Look for robotics clubs near you. There may be one at your school or opportunites to develop your skills in maths and science lessons. Perhaps you will design the robots of the future. The possibilities are endless!

# GLOSSARY

**axle**  bar in the centre of a wheel around which a wheel turns

**battery**  device that uses chemical reactions to make electricity

**bearing**  in machinery, a part that allows moving parts to work with as little wear and tear as possible

**circuit**  path for electricity to flow through

**code**  system of words, letters, symbols or numbers used instead of ordinary words to send messages or store information; computer code serves as instructions for a computer

**convert**  change from one thing to another; energy can be converted from one type to another

**electron**  negatively charged particle that whirls around the nucleus of an atom

**microprocessor**  tiny computer processor contained in an electronic computer chip

**precision**  with exact accuracy

**sensor**  instrument that detects changes and sends information to a controlling device

**tension**  stress on a structure resulting from stretching or pulling

**voltage**  force of an electrical current; voltage is measured in volts

# READ MORE

*Incredible Robots in Medicine* (Incredible Robots), Louise and Richard Spilsbury (Raintree, 2017)

*Mars Rover Driver* (The Coolest Jobs on the Planet), Scott Maxwell (Raintree, 2014)

*The Usborne Science Encyclopedia,* Kirsteen Robson (Usborne Publishing Ltd, 2015)

# WEBSITES

**www.bbc.co.uk/education/clips/z362xnb**
Watch this video about robots that have been programmed to play football!

**www.dkfindout.com/uk/computer-coding/what-is-coding/**
Find out more about computer code and programming.

# INDEX

# AUTHOR BIO

Ed Sobey, PhD, is a world explorer with numerous scientific expeditions. He holds a PhD in oceanography and teaches oceanography, and weather and climate for Semester at Sea.

Ed is a global evangelist for creative learning. He encourages creativity, inventing and innovation through his books, workshops and travelling museum exhibits throughout the world. The Institute for International Education has awarded Ed two Fulbright grants for science teaching. Teachers in more than 30 countries have participated in his workshops.

He was the founding director of the National Inventors Hall of Fame in the United States, as well as being founder of the National Toy Hall of Fame and co-founder of Kids Invent! He has directed five museums in the United States and has served as President of the Ohio Museums Association. He has also hosted two television programmes on science for children and young people.